Oster Blender Cookbook for Beginners

600 Gluten-Free, Vegan Recipes for Fast, Healthy Meals

Gulre Saphor

Table of Contents

Introduction

The Oster Blender is one of the most popular and top-selling models of the powerful blender available in the market.

This cookbook contains healthy and delicious Oster blender recipes that come from different categories like Appetizers, soups, salsas, dressings, sauces, spreads, desserts, and drinks. The recipes written in this book are unique and written into an easily understandable form. All the recipes start with their preparation and cooking (blending) time followed by step-by-step instructions. At the end of each recipe, nutritional value information is written. The nutritional value information will help to keep track of daily calorie intake. There various books available in the market on this topic thanks for choosing my cookbook. I hope you love and enjoy all the recipes written in this book.

Chapter 1: Appetizers

Lemon Garlic Pistachio Dip

Preparation Time: 5 minutes
Cooking Time: 1 minute
Serve: 8

Ingredients:

- 1/4 cup pistachios
- 1 cup shelled edamame, cooked
- 1/2 cup water
- 2 tbsp olive oil
- 1 fresh lemon juice
- 1 garlic clove
- 1/2 cup fresh parsley
- Pepper
- Salt

Directions:

1. Add all ingredients into the blender container. Secure the lid.
2. Start the blending at low speed, then quickly increase to highest speed and blend for 1 minute or until getting the desired consistency.
3. Serve and enjoy.

Nutritional Value (Amount per Serving):

- Calories 64
- Fat 5.4 g
- Carbohydrates 2.4 g
- Sugar 0.6 g
- Protein 2.3 g
- Cholesterol 0 mg

Creamy Spinach Dip

Preparation Time: 5 minutes
Cooking Time: 1 minute
Serve: 12

Ingredients:

- 10 oz frozen spinach, thawed & drained
- 1/2 tsp garlic powder
- 1/4 tsp cayenne
- 8 oz sour cream
- 1 tbsp fresh lime juice

Directions:

1. Add all ingredients into the blender container. Secure the lid.
2. Start the blending at low speed, then quickly increase to highest speed and blend until smooth.
3. Serve and enjoy.

Nutritional Value (Amount per Serving):

- Calories 339
- Fat 10 g
- Carbohydrates 56.1 g
- Sugar 22 g
- Protein 7.5 g
- Cholesterol 76 mg

Easy Avocado Dip

Preparation Time: 5 minutes
Cooking Time: 1 minute
Serve: 6

Ingredients:

- 2 avocados, scoop out the flesh
- 1/4 tsp onion powder
- 1/2 cup Greek yogurt
- 1 lemon juice
- 1 cup fresh cilantro
- 2 garlic cloves
- Pepper
- Salt

Directions:

1. Add all ingredients into the blender container. Secure the lid.
2. Start the blending at low speed, then quickly increase to highest speed and blend until smooth.
3. Serve and enjoy.

Nutritional Value (Amount per Serving):

- Calories 154
- Fat 13.5 g
- Carbohydrates 7.1 g
- Sugar 1.2 g
- Protein 3.1 g
- Cholesterol 1 mg

Roasted Pepper Hummus

Preparation Time: 5 minutes
Cooking Time: 1 minute
Serve: 8

Ingredients:

- 15 oz can chickpeas, drain
- 1 tsp ground cumin
- 4 garlic cloves
- 1 tbsp tahini
- 1/4 cup fresh lemon juice
- 1/2 cup roasted red peppers, drained
- 1/4 cup vegetable broth
- Pepper
- Salt

Directions:

1. Add all ingredients into the blender container. Secure the lid.
2. Start the blending at low speed, then quickly increase to highest speed and blend until smooth.
3. Serve and enjoy.

Nutritional Value (Amount per Serving):

- Calories 83
- Fat 1.8 g
- Carbohydrates 13.8 g
- Sugar 0.7 g
- Protein 3.4 g
- Cholesterol 0 mg

Cashew Queso Dip

Preparation Time: 5 minutes
Cooking Time: 1 minute
Serve: 8

Ingredients:

- 1 cup cashews
- 1/2 tsp chili powder
- 1 garlic clove
- 1/2 tsp paprika
- 1 tsp onion powder
- 1/3 cup marinara sauce
- 3/4 cup hot water
- Pepper
- Salt

Directions:

1. Add all ingredients into the blender container. Secure the lid.
2. Start the blending at low speed, then quickly increase to highest speed and blend until smooth.
3. Serve and enjoy.

Nutritional Value (Amount per Serving):

- Calories 110
- Fat 8.3 g
- Carbohydrates 7.6 g
- Sugar 1.9 g
- Protein 2.9 g
- Cholesterol 0 mg

Flavorful Salsa Dip

Preparation Time: 5 minutes
Cooking Time: 1 minute
Serve: 10

Ingredients:

- 1 cup salsa
- 1 cup fresh cilantro
- 2 tsp taco seasoning
- 3/4 cup sour cream

Directions:

1. Add all ingredients into the blender container. Secure the lid.
2. Start the blending at low speed, then quickly increase to highest speed and blend until smooth.
3. Serve and enjoy.

Nutritional Value (Amount per Serving):

- Calories 119
- Fat 7.8 g
- Carbohydrates 7.8 g
- Sugar 0.8 g
- Protein 5.1 g
- Cholesterol 19 mg

Cannellini Bean Dip

Preparation Time: 5 minutes
Cooking Time: 1 minute
Serve: 8

Ingredients:

- 1 cup can cannellini beans, drained
- 4 tbsp tahini
- 1 lemon juice
- 1 1/2 tsp ground cumin
- 1/4 cup olive oil
- 1/4 cup water
- 2 garlic cloves
- 1 cup can chickpeas, drained
- Salt

Directions:

1. Add all ingredients into the blender container. Secure the lid.
2. Start the blending at low speed, then quickly increase to highest speed and blend until smooth.
3. Serve and enjoy.

Nutritional Value (Amount per Serving):

- Calories 168
- Fat 10.8 g
- Carbohydrates 14.2 g
- Sugar 0.4 g
- Protein 4.9 g
- Cholesterol 0 mg

Spicy Chipotle Ranch Dip

Preparation Time: 5 minutes
Cooking Time: 1 minute
Serve: 4

Ingredients:

- 2 chipotle peppers in adobo sauce
- 3 tbsp water
- 1 garlic clove
- 1/2 tbsp fresh lime juice
- 1 tsp dried dill
- 1/2 tsp onion powder
- 1 1/2 tsp garlic powder
- 1/2 cup Greek yogurt
- 1/2 cup mayonnaise
- Pepper
- Salt

Directions:

1. Add all ingredients into the blender container. Secure the lid.
2. Start the blending at low speed, then quickly increase to highest speed and blend until smooth.
3. Serve and enjoy.

Nutritional Value (Amount per Serving):

- Calories 154
- Fat 10.6 g
- Carbohydrates 12.9 g
- Sugar 4.4 g
- Protein 3.1 g
- Cholesterol 9 mg

Easy Jalapeno Ranch Dip

Preparation Time: 5 minutes
Cooking Time: 1 minute
Serve: 4

Ingredients:

- 8 oz can jalapeno peppers with juice
- 1 cup sour cream
- 1 cup mayonnaise
- 1/2 tsp garlic powder
- 1/4 cup fresh cilantro
- 1/2 tsp pepper
- 1 tsp salt

Directions:

1. Add all ingredients into the blender container. Secure the lid.
2. Start the blending at low speed, then quickly increase to highest speed and blend until smooth.
3. Serve and enjoy.

Nutritional Value (Amount per Serving):

- Calories 354
- Fat 31.7 g
- Carbohydrates 17 g
- Sugar 4 g
- Protein 2.5 g
- Cholesterol 41 mg

Easy Olive Tapenade

Preparation Time: 5 minutes
Cooking Time: 1 minute
Serve: 4

Ingredients:

- 2 cups olives, pitted
- 1/4 cup olive oil
- 1 tbsp fresh lemon juice
- 2 tbsp parsley
- 1 tbsp fresh basil
- 2 garlic cloves
- 1 tbsp capers
- 1/4 cup sun-dried tomatoes, drained

Directions:

1. Add all ingredients into the blender container. Secure the lid.
2. Start the blending at low speed, then quickly increase to highest speed and blend for 1 minute or until getting the desired consistency.
3. Serve and enjoy.

Nutritional Value (Amount per Serving):

- Calories 192
- Fat 19.9 g
- Carbohydrates 5.5 g
- Sugar 0.4 g
- Protein 0.9 g
- Cholesterol 0 mg

Roasted Pepper Dip

Preparation Time: 5 minutes
Cooking Time: 1 minute
Serve: 12

Ingredients:

- 16 oz roasted red bell peppers, drained
- 1/4 tsp red pepper flakes
- 1 tsp paprika
- 1 tbsp honey
- 1 tbsp lime juice
- 1 tbsp extra-virgin olive oil
- 2 garlic cloves
- 1 1/2 cups walnuts, roasted
- Salt

Directions:

1. Add all ingredients into the blender container. Secure the lid.
2. Start the blending at low speed, then quickly increase to highest speed and blend until smooth.
3. Serve and enjoy.

Nutritional Value (Amount per Serving):

- Calories 138
- Fat 12.2 g
- Carbohydrates 7.1 g
- Sugar 2.9 g
- Protein 5 g
- Cholesterol 0 mg

Flavorful Cranberry Salsa

Preparation Time: 5 minutes
Cooking Time: 1 minute
Serve: 8

Ingredients:

- 12 oz fresh cranberries
- 2 jalapeno peppers, chopped
- 1/4 cup fresh cilantro
- 1 tbsp orange zest
- 2 tbsp ginger, chopped
- 2 tbsp fresh lemon juice
- 1/2 cup sugar
- Pinch of salt

Directions:

1. Add all ingredients into the blender container. Secure the lid.
2. Start the blending at low speed, then quickly increase to highest speed and blend until getting chunky consistency.
3. Pour blended mixture into the bowl and place in the refrigerator for 5-6 hours.
4. Serve and enjoy.

Nutritional Value (Amount per Serving):

- Calories 78
- Fat 0.2 g
- Carbohydrates 17.9 g
- Sugar 14.3 g
- Protein 0.2 g
- Cholesterol 0 mg

Healthy Beetroot Dip

Preparation Time: 5 minutes
Cooking Time: 1 minute
Serve: 8

Ingredients:

- 1 cup pickled beets, drain the liquid
- 20 oz can white beans, drained
- 1 1/2 tbsp vinegar
- 1/4 cup olive oil
- 2 garlic cloves
- 3 tbsp fresh lemon juice
- 1 tbsp lemon zest
- 1/3 cup tahini
- 1/2 tsp salt

Directions:

1. Add all ingredients into the blender container. Secure the lid.
2. Start the blending at low speed, then quickly increase to highest speed and blend until smooth.
3. Serve and enjoy.

Nutritional Value (Amount per Serving):

- Calories 207
- Fat 11.9 g
- Carbohydrates 22.4 g
- Sugar 4.4 g
- Protein 7.2 g
- Cholesterol 0 mg

Creamy Feta Dip

Preparation Time: 5 minutes
Cooking Time: 1 minute
Serve: 4

Ingredients:

- 7 oz feta cheese, drained
- 1/2 tsp lemon zest
- 1 tbsp olive oil
- 1/2 cup sour cream
- Pepper
- Salt

Directions:

1. Add all ingredients into the blender container. Secure the lid.
2. Start the blending at low speed, then quickly increase to highest speed and blend until smooth & creamy.
3. Serve and enjoy.

Nutritional Value (Amount per Serving):

- Calories 223
- Fat 20.1 g
- Carbohydrates 3.3 g
- Sugar 2.1 g
- Protein 8 g
- Cholesterol 57 mg

Avocado Salsa Dip

Preparation Time: 5 minutes
Cooking Time: 1 minute
Serve: 12

Ingredients:

- 2 avocados, scoop out the flesh
- 1/4 tsp ground cumin
- 1/2 tsp garlic powder
- 1 garlic clove
- 1/3 cup onion, chopped
- 1/2 cup cilantro
- 1 lime juice
- 1 jalapeno pepper
- 10 oz tomatillos
- Salt

Directions:

1. Add all ingredients into the blender container. Secure the lid.
2. Start the blending at low speed, then quickly increase to highest speed and blend for 1 minute or until getting the desired consistency.
3. Serve and enjoy.

Nutritional Value (Amount per Serving):

- Calories 80
- Fat 6.8 g
- Carbohydrates 5.2 g
- Sugar 0.5 g
- Protein 1 g
- Cholesterol 0 mg

Quick & Easy Black Bean Dip

Preparation Time: 5 minutes
Cooking Time: 1 minute
Serve: 8

Ingredients:

- 30 oz can black beans, drained
- 1/4 tsp onion powder
- 1/4 tsp smoked paprika
- 1/4 tsp ground cumin
- 1/2 tsp chili powder
- 1 1/2 tsp garlic, minced
- 1 tbsp fresh lime juice
- 1/2 cup fire-roasted tomatoes, diced
- 1/2 tsp salt

Directions:

1. Add all ingredients into the blender container. Secure the lid.
2. Start the blending at low speed, then quickly increase to highest speed and blend for 1 minute or until getting the desired consistency.
3. Serve and enjoy.

Nutritional Value (Amount per Serving):

- Calories 105
- Fat 0.8 g
- Carbohydrates 19.7 g
- Sugar 1.2 g
- Protein 5.8 g
- Cholesterol 0 mg

Creamy Avocado Dip

Preparation Time: 5 minutes
Cooking Time: 1 minute
Serve: 6

Ingredients:

- 1 avocado, scoop out the flesh
- 1 lime juice
- 2 tbsp water
- 1 garlic clove
- 1/2 cup fresh cilantro
- 1/3 cup mayonnaise

Directions:

1. Add all ingredients into the blender container. Secure the lid.
2. Start the blending at low speed, then quickly increase to highest speed and blend until smooth.
3. Serve and enjoy.

Nutritional Value (Amount per Serving):

- Calories 122
- Fat 10.9 g
- Carbohydrates 6.8 g
- Sugar 1.2 g
- Protein 0.9 g
- Cholesterol 3 mg

Quick Olive Dip

Preparation Time: 5 minutes
Cooking Time: 1 minute
Serve: 8

Ingredients:

- 6 oz green olives, drained
- 16 oz cream cheese, softened
- 1/2 tsp garlic powder
- 1/2 tsp onion powder
- 1/2 cup mayonnaise

Directions:

1. Add all ingredients into the blender container. Secure the lid.
2. Start the blending at low speed, then quickly increase to highest speed and blend for 1 minute or until getting the desired consistency.
3. Serve and enjoy.

Nutritional Value (Amount per Serving):

- Calories 274
- Fat 26.1 g
- Carbohydrates 6.5 g
- Sugar 1.1 g
- Protein 4.7 g
- Cholesterol 66 mg

Lemon Pepper Cheese Dip

Preparation Time: 5 minutes
Cooking Time: 1 minute
Serve: 8

Ingredients:

- 4 oz Asiago cheese, cubed
- 1/2 lemon juice
- 1 lemon zest
- 2 garlic cloves
- 1 tbsp thyme, minced
- 6 tbsp sour cream
- 1 oz parmesan cheese
- 1/2 tsp pepper
- 1/4 tsp salt

Directions:

1. Add all ingredients into the blender container. Secure the lid.
2. Start the blending at low speed, then quickly increase to highest speed and blend until smooth.
3. Serve and enjoy.

Nutritional Value (Amount per Serving):

- Calories 85
- Fat 6.8 g
- Carbohydrates 1.2 g
- Sugar 0.1 g
- Protein 5.1 g
- Cholesterol 19 mg

Perfect Artichoke Dip

Preparation Time: 5 minutes
Cooking Time: 1 minute
Serve: 4

Ingredients:

- 14 oz can artichoke hearts, drained
- 2 tbsp water
- 1 tsp chili powder
- 2 garlic cloves
- 1 tbsp lemon juice
- 2 tbsp olive oil
- 2 tbsp tahini
- 1/4 cup nutritional yeast
- 15 oz can chickpeas, drained
- Pepper
- Salt

Directions:

1. Add all ingredients into the blender container. Secure the lid.
2. Start the blending at low speed, then quickly increase to highest speed and blend for 1 minute or until getting the desired consistency.
3. Serve and enjoy.

Nutritional Value (Amount per Serving):

- Calories 301
- Fat 12.9 g
- Carbohydrates 36.1 g
- Sugar 1 g
- Protein 13 g
- Cholesterol 0 mg

Cauliflower Artichoke Dip

Preparation Time: 5 minutes
Cooking Time: 1 minute
Serve: 8

Ingredients:

- 2 cups artichoke hearts
- 1/2 cup cauliflower florets, cooked
- 3 cups spinach, chopped
- 2 tsp nutritional yeast
- 1/3 cup vegetable broth
- 1/2 cup coconut cream, softened
- 3 garlic cloves, minced
- 1 onion, diced
- 2 tbsp olive oil
- 1 tsp salt

Directions:

1. Add all ingredients into the blender container. Secure the lid.
2. Start the blending at low speed, then quickly increase to highest speed and blend for 1 minute or until getting the desired consistency.
3. Serve and enjoy.

Nutritional Value (Amount per Serving):

- Calories 95
- Fat 7.3 g
- Carbohydrates 7 g
- Sugar 1.6 g
- Protein 2.6 g
- Cholesterol 0 mg

Corn Salsa

Preparation Time: 5 minutes
Cooking Time: 1 minute
Serve: 4

Ingredients:

- 1 cup corn kernels, thawed
- 1/2 cup scallions, chopped
- 1 lime juice
- 1 jalapeno, chopped
- 1/4 cup fresh cilantro
- 2 small tomatoes, chopped
- Salt

Directions:

1. Add all ingredients into the blender container. Secure the lid.
2. Start the blending at low speed, then quickly increase to highest speed and blend until getting chunky consistency.
3. Serve and enjoy.

Nutritional Value (Amount per Serving):

- Calories 49
- Fat 0.6 g
- Carbohydrates 11.1 g
- Sugar 3.1 g
- Protein 2 g
- Cholesterol 0 mg

Chapter 2: Soups & Salsas

Creamy Asparagus Soup

Preparation Time: 5 minutes
Cooking Time: 6 minutes
Serve: 4

Ingredients:

- 1 lb asparagus, cooked and chopped
- 2 garlic cloves
- 1 onion, diced
- 3 1/4 cups vegetable stock
- 1 tbsp olive oil
- 1 tbsp fresh lemon juice
- 1 leek, sliced
- Pepper
- Salt

Directions:

1. Add all ingredients into the blender container. Secure the lid.
2. Start the blending at low speed, then quickly increase to highest speed and blend for 6 minutes.
3. Serve and enjoy.

Nutritional Value (Amount per Serving):

- Calories 85
- Fat 3.9 g
- Carbohydrates 11.5 g
- Sugar 4.8 g
- Protein 3.6 g
- Cholesterol 0 mg

Spicy Squash Soup

Preparation Time: 5 minutes
Cooking Time: 6 minutes
Serve: 4

Ingredients:

- 1 butternut squash, cut into chunks
- 1 potato, peel, cook, and chopped
- 1 onion, chopped
- 1 red chili, chopped
- 3 garlic cloves, peeled
- 3 cups vegetable stock
- Pepper
- Salt

Directions:

1. Add all ingredients into the blender container. Secure the lid.
2. Start the blending at low speed, then quickly increase to highest speed and blend for 6 minutes.
3. Serve and enjoy.

Nutritional Value (Amount per Serving):

- Calories 68
- Fat 0.2 g
- Carbohydrates 15.6 g
- Sugar 2.9 g
- Protein 2 g
- Cholesterol 0 mg

Tomato Pepper Soup

Preparation Time: 5 minutes
Cooking Time: 6 minutes
Serve: 4

Ingredients:

- 1 lb fresh tomatoes, halved
- 3 garlic cloves
- 2 cups vegetable stock
- 14 oz can tomatoes
- 1 onion, sliced
- 2 peppers, sliced
- 1 tbsp olive oil
- 1 1/2 tsp red chili flakes
- Pepper
- Salt

Directions:

1. Add all ingredients into the blender container. Secure the lid.
2. Start the blending at low speed, then quickly increase to highest speed and blend for 6 minutes.
3. Serve and enjoy.

Nutritional Value (Amount per Serving):

- Calories 90
- Fat 3.8 g
- Carbohydrates 13.6 g
- Sugar 7.9 g
- Protein 2.6 g
- Cholesterol 0 mg

Tomatillo Pineapple Salsa

Preparation Time: 5 minutes
Cooking Time: 1 minute
Serve: 8

Ingredients:

- 1 cup pineapple, diced
- 1 jalapeno pepper
- 1 lb tomatillos, husks removed & chopped
- 1 cup water
- 1/2 lime juice
- 1/2 cup cilantro
- 4.5 green chilies, diced
- 1/2 onion, chopped
- 1/2 tsp salt

Directions:

1. Add all ingredients into the blender container. Secure the lid.
2. Start the blending at low speed, then slowly increase speed to variable 3 and blend for 15-20 seconds or until getting the desired consistency.
3. Serve and enjoy.

Nutritional Value (Amount per Serving):

- Calories 34
- Fat 0.7 g
- Carbohydrates 7.2 g
- Sugar 2.6 g
- Protein 0.8 g
- Cholesterol 0 mg

Broccoli Soup

Preparation Time: 5 minutes
Cooking Time: 6 minutes
Serve: 4

Ingredients:

- 4 cups broccoli florets, boil & drained
- 3 garlic cloves
- 6 cup vegetable stock
- 1 tsp thyme
- 1 potato, peel, cooked, and cubed
- 1/2 tsp onion powder
- Pepper
- Salt

Directions:

1. Add all ingredients into the blender container. Secure the lid.
2. Start the blending at low speed, then quickly increase to highest speed and blend for 6 minutes.
3. Serve and enjoy.

Nutritional Value (Amount per Serving):

- Calories 78
- Fat 0.5 g
- Carbohydrates 16 g
- Sugar 3.1 g
- Protein 4.2 g
- Cholesterol 0 mg

Creamy Squash Soup

Preparation Time: 5 minutes
Cooking Time: 6 minutes
Serve: 6

Ingredients:

- 6 cups butternut squash, peel, cook, and cubed
- 2 tsp thyme
- 1/4 cup heavy cream
- 3 cups vegetable stock
- 1 onion, chopped
- 1/8 tsp nutmeg
- 2 tbsp olive oil
- 1/8 tsp cayenne
- Pepper
- Salt

Directions:

1. Add all ingredients into the blender container. Secure the lid.
2. Start the blending at low speed, then quickly increase to highest speed and blend for 6 minutes.
3. Serve and enjoy.

Nutritional Value (Amount per Serving):

- Calories 132
- Fat 6.8 g
- Carbohydrates 18.9 g
- Sugar 4.2 g
- Protein 1.9 g
- Cholesterol 7 mg

Cauliflower Soup

Preparation Time: 5 minutes
Cooking Time: 6 minutes
Serve: 4

Ingredients:

- 2 cups cauliflower florets, boiled & drained
- 1 tsp pumpkin pie spice
- 1 onion, chopped
- 5 cups vegetable broth
- 3 tbsp olive oil
- Pepper
- Salt

Directions:

1. Add all ingredients into the blender container. Secure the lid.
2. Start the blending at low speed, then quickly increase to highest speed and blend for 6 minutes.
3. Serve and enjoy.

Nutritional Value (Amount per Serving):

- Calories 163
- Fat 12.3 g
- Carbohydrates 6.7 g
- Sugar 3.3 g
- Protein 7.4 g
- Cholesterol 0 mg

Berry Salsa

Preparation Time: 5 minutes
Cooking Time: 1 minute
Serve: 8

Ingredients:

- 8 strawberries
- 2 cups blueberries
- 1 lime juice
- 1 jalapeno pepper
- 1/4 cup cilantro
- Salt

Directions:

1. Add all ingredients into the blender container. Secure the lid.
2. Start the blending at low speed, then slowly increase speed to variable 3 and blend for 15-20 seconds or until getting the desired consistency.
3. Serve and enjoy.

Nutritional Value (Amount per Serving):

- Calories 25
- Fat 0.2 g
- Carbohydrates 6.3 g
- Sugar 4.3 g
- Protein 0.4 g
- Cholesterol 0 mg

Potato Leek Soup

Preparation Time: 5 minutes
Cooking Time: 6 minutes
Serve: 4

Ingredients:

- 1 lb potatoes, peel, cooked, and chopped
- 1 onion, chopped
- 1 cup leek, chopped
- 3 cups vegetable stock
- 1/2 cup fresh cream
- Pepper
- Salt

Directions:

1. Add all ingredients into the blender container. Secure the lid.
2. Start the blending at low speed, then quickly increase to highest speed and blend for 6 minutes.
3. Serve and enjoy.

Nutritional Value (Amount per Serving):

- Calories 127
- Fat 2 g
- Carbohydrates 25.2 g
- Sugar 4.5 g
- Protein 3.1 g
- Cholesterol 6 mg

Delicious Cranberry Salsa

Preparation Time: 5 minutes
Cooking Time: 1 minute
Serve: 8

Ingredients:

- 12 oz cranberries
- 2 jalapeno pepper, chopped
- 1/4 cup cilantro
- 1 tbsp lemon zest
- 1 1/2 tbsp ginger, chopped
- 2 tbsp lime juice
- 1/2 cup sugar

Directions:

1. Add all ingredients into the blender container. Secure the lid.
2. Start the blending at low speed, then slowly increase speed to variable 3 and blend for 15-20 seconds or until getting the desired consistency.
3. Serve and enjoy.

Nutritional Value (Amount per Serving):

- Calories 78
- Fat 0.1 g
- Carbohydrates 18.4 g
- Sugar 14.2 g
- Protein 0.2 g
- Cholesterol 0 mg

Strawberry Salsa

Preparation Time: 5 minutes
Cooking Time: 1 minute
Serve: 4

Ingredients:

- 1 cup strawberries
- 1/4 cup cilantro
- 1 lime juice
- 1 jalapeno pepper
- 1/4 onion

Directions:

1. Add all ingredients into the blender container. Secure the lid.
2. Start the blending at low speed, then slowly increase speed to variable 3 and blend for 15-20 seconds or until getting chunky consistency.
3. Serve and enjoy.

Nutritional Value (Amount per Serving):

- Calories 18
- Fat 0.2 g
- Carbohydrates 4.6 g
- Sugar 2.4 g
- Protein 0.4 g
- Cholesterol 0 mg

Easy Onion Soup

Preparation Time: 5 minutes
Cooking Time: 6 minutes
Serve: 6

Ingredients:

- 8 cups onions, peel and slice
- 6 cups vegetable broth
- 2 tbsp olive oil
- 1/4 tsp garlic powder
- 1 tbsp balsamic vinegar
- Pepper
- Salt

Directions:

1. Add all ingredients into the blender container. Secure the lid.
2. Start the blending at low speed, then quickly increase to highest speed and blend for 6 minutes.
3. Serve and enjoy.

Nutritional Value (Amount per Serving):

- Calories 141
- Fat 6.2 g
- Carbohydrates 15.4 g
- Sugar 7.2 g
- Protein 6.6 g
- Cholesterol 0 mg

Tasty Garden Salsa

Preparation Time: 5 minutes
Cooking Time: 1 minute
Serve: 8

Ingredients:

- 5 tomatoes, halved
- 2 garlic cloves
- 1 lime juice
- 1 jalapeno pepper
- 1/2 onion
- 1/2 tsp sugar
- Pepper
- Salt

Directions:

1. Add all ingredients into the blender container. Secure the lid.
2. Start the blending at low speed, then slowly increase speed to variable 3 and blend for 15-20 seconds or until getting the desired consistency.
3. Serve and enjoy.

Nutritional Value (Amount per Serving):

- Calories 21
- Fat 0.2 g
- Carbohydrates 4.7 g
- Sugar 2.7 g
- Protein 0.9 g
- Cholesterol 0 mg

Mango Salsa

Preparation Time: 5 minutes
Cooking Time: 1 minute
Serve: 8

Ingredients:

- 1 1/2 cups mangoes, diced
- 1/3 cup green onion, chopped
- 1 bell pepper, diced
- 1 lime juice
- 1 jalapeno pepper, diced
- 1/2 cup cilantro
- Salt

Directions:

1. Add all ingredients into the blender container. Secure the lid.
2. Start the blending at low speed, then slowly increase speed to variable 3 and blend for 15-20 seconds or until getting the desired consistency.
3. Serve and enjoy.

Nutritional Value (Amount per Serving):

- Calories 25
- Fat 0.2 g
- Carbohydrates 6.7 g
- Sugar 5.2 g
- Protein 0.5 g
- Cholesterol 0 mg

Chapter 3: Dressing, Sauces & Spreads

Creamy Avocado Dressing

Preparation Time: 10 minutes
Cooking Time: 1 minute
Serve: 4

Ingredients:

- 1 avocado, scoop out the flesh
- 1 garlic clove
- 1 lemon juice
- 2 tbsp water
- 1/4 cup olive oil
- 1/2 cup cilantro
- Pepper
- Salt

Directions:

1. Add all ingredients into the blender container. Secure the lid.
2. Start the blending at low speed, then quickly increase to highest speed and blend for 1 minute or until smooth.
3. Serve and enjoy.

Nutritional Value (Amount per Serving):

- Calories 215
- Fat 22.5 g
- Carbohydrates 4.9 g
- Sugar 0.5 g
- Protein 1.1 g
- Cholesterol 0 mg

Mango Mustard Sauce

Preparation Time: 10 minutes
Cooking Time: 1 minute
Serve: 4

Ingredients:

- 1/2 cup mango, chopped
- 1 tbsp fresh lemon juice
- 1 tsp red chili flakes
- 2 1/2 tbsp Dijon mustard
- 1/4 cup mayonnaise
- Salt

Directions:

1. Add all ingredients into the blender container. Secure the lid.
2. Start the blending at low speed, then quickly increase to highest speed and blend for 1 minute or until smooth.
3. Serve and enjoy.

Nutritional Value (Amount per Serving):

- Calories 77
- Fat 5.4 g
- Carbohydrates 7.2 g
- Sugar 3.9 g
- Protein 0.8 g
- Cholesterol 4 mg

Creamy Avocado Sauce

Preparation Time: 10 minutes
Cooking Time: 1 minute
Serve: 8

Ingredients:

- 1 avocado, scoop out the flesh
- 2 tbsp fresh lemon juice
- 4 oz sour cream
- 1/4 tsp garlic powder
- Pepper
- Salt

Directions:

1. Add all ingredients into the blender container. Secure the lid.
2. Start the blending at low speed, then quickly increase to highest speed and blend for 1 minute or until smooth.
3. Serve and enjoy.

Nutritional Value (Amount per Serving):

- Calories 83
- Fat 7.9 g
- Carbohydrates 2.9 g
- Sugar 0.3 g
- Protein 1 g
- Cholesterol 6 mg

Classic Caesar Dressing

Preparation Time: 10 minutes
Cooking Time: 1 minute
Serve: 4

Ingredients:

- 1/2 cup olive oil
- 1 tsp Dijon mustard
- 2 tbsp fresh lime juice
- 1/3 cup parmesan cheese, grated
- 2 egg yolks
- 1 garlic clove
- 4 anchovy fillets, drained
- Pepper
- Salt

Directions:

1. Add all ingredients into the blender container. Secure the lid.
2. Start the blending at low speed, then quickly increase to highest speed and blend for 1 minute or until smooth.
3. Serve and enjoy.

Nutritional Value (Amount per Serving):

- Calories 266
- Fat 28.4 g
- Carbohydrates 2.6 g
- Sugar 0.4 g
- Protein 3.5 g
- Cholesterol 110 mg

Chipotle Sauce

Preparation Time: 10 minutes
Cooking Time: 1 minute
Serve: 10

Ingredients:

- 7 oz can chipotle peppers in adobo sauce
- 1/2 cup cilantro
- 3/4 tsp garlic powder
- 1 tsp ground cumin
- 1 tsp chili powder
- 4 tbsp mayonnaise
- 1/2 cup Greek yogurt
- Salt

Directions:

1. Add all ingredients into the blender container. Secure the lid.
2. Start the blending at low speed, then quickly increase to highest speed and blend for 1 minute or until smooth.
3. Serve and enjoy.

Nutritional Value (Amount per Serving):

- Calories 53
- Fat 3.2 g
- Carbohydrates 4.9 g
- Sugar 2.8 g
- Protein 1.9 g
- Cholesterol 2 mg

Delicious Tahini Dressing

Preparation Time: 10 minutes
Cooking Time: 1 minute
Serve: 8

Ingredients:

- 1/2 cup tahini
- 1 garlic clove
- 1 tsp onion powder
- 1 tsp vinegar
- 1 tsp Dijon mustard
- 1 tbsp fresh dill
- 1 tbsp fresh chives
- 3 tbsp lemon juice
- 1/2 cup water
- Salt

Directions:

1. Add all ingredients into the blender container. Secure the lid.
2. Start the blending at low speed, then quickly increase to highest speed and blend for 1 minute or until smooth.
3. Serve and enjoy.

Nutritional Value (Amount per Serving):

- Calories 94
- Fat 8.2 g
- Carbohydrates 4 g
- Sugar 0.3 g
- Protein 2.8 g

Cholesterol 0 mgVegan Greek Dressing

Preparation Time: 10 minutes
Cooking Time: 1 minute
Serve: 8

Ingredients:

- 1 cup olive oil
- 1/4 tsp red chili flakes
- 1/4 cup parsley
- 1 tbsp Dijon mustard
- 1 tsp dried basil
- 1 tsp dried oregano
- 2 garlic cloves
- 1/3 cup water
- 1/2 cup vinegar
- Pepper
- Salt

Directions:

1. Add all ingredients into the blender container. Secure the lid.
2. Start the blending at low speed, then quickly increase to highest speed and blend for 1 minute or until smooth.
3. Serve and enjoy.

Nutritional Value (Amount per Serving):

- Calories 223
- Fat 25.3 g
- Carbohydrates 0.7 g
- Sugar 0.1 g
- Protein 0.2 g
- Cholesterol 0 mg

Southwest Dressing

Preparation Time: 10 minutes
Cooking Time: 1 minute
Serve: 8

Ingredients:

- 1/4 tsp chipotle powder
- 1/2 tsp paprika
- 1/2 tsp dill
- 1 tsp ground cumin
- 1 tsp onion powder
- 1 tsp garlic powder
- 1 1/2 tsp chili powder
- 1/4 cup fresh lemon juice
- 1 cup mayonnaise
- Salt

Directions:

1. Add all ingredients into the blender container. Secure the lid.
2. Start the blending at low speed, then quickly increase to highest speed and blend for 1 minute or until smooth.
3. Serve and enjoy.

Nutritional Value (Amount per Serving):

- Calories 138
- Fat 11.8 g
- Carbohydrates 8.3 g
- Sugar 2.4 g
- Protein 0.6 g
- Cholesterol 9 mg

Mango Lemon Dressing

Preparation Time: 10 minutes
Cooking Time: 1 minute
Serve: 6

Ingredients:

- 1 cup mango, diced
- 1/2 tsp garlic powder
- 1/2 tsp ground cumin
- 1/4 cup cilantro
- 1 tbsp olive oil
- 1 tbsp vinegar
- 1 lemon juice
- Salt

Directions:

1. Add all ingredients into the blender container. Secure the lid.
2. Start the blending at low speed, then quickly increase to highest speed and blend for 1 minute or until smooth.
3. Serve and enjoy.

Nutritional Value (Amount per Serving):

- Calories 41
- Fat 2.5 g
- Carbohydrates 4.6 g
- Sugar 4 g
- Protein 0.4 g
- Cholesterol 0 mg

Chimichurri Sauce

Preparation Time: 10 minutes
Cooking Time: 1 minute
Serve: 8

Ingredients:

- 1 jalapeno pepper
- 1 small onion, quartered
- 4 garlic cloves
- 2 tsp dried oregano
- 1/2 cup fresh cilantro
- 1/2 cup fresh parsley
- 1/2 cup vinegar
- 1/2 cup extra-virgin olive oil
- Pepper
- Salt

Directions:

1. Add all ingredients into the blender container. Secure the lid.
2. Start the blending at low speed, then quickly increase to highest speed and blend for 1 minute or until smooth.
3. Serve and enjoy.

Nutritional Value (Amount per Serving):

- Calories 120
- Fat 12.7 g
- Carbohydrates 2.1 g
- Sugar 0.6 g
- Protein 0.4 g
- Cholesterol 0 mg

Low-carb BBQ Sauce

Preparation Time: 10 minutes
Cooking Time: 1 minute
Serve: 4

Ingredients:

- 6 oz can tomato paste
- 1 tsp Dijon mustard
- 1/2 tsp chipotle powder
- 3/4 tsp paprika
- 1 tsp garlic powder
- 1 tbsp onion powder
- 1/2 cup Swerve
- 2 tbsp water
- 1/4 cup vinegar
- 1 tsp salt

Directions:

1. Add all ingredients into the blender container. Secure the lid.
2. Start the blending at low speed, then quickly increase to highest speed and blend for 1 minute or until smooth.
3. Serve and enjoy.

Nutritional Value (Amount per Serving):

- Calories 49
- Fat 0.4 g
- Carbohydrates 10.6 g
- Sugar 6.1 g
- Protein 2.3 g
- Cholesterol 0 mg

Avocado Sandwich Spread

Preparation Time: 10 minutes
Cooking Time: 1 minute
Serve: 2

Ingredients:

- 1 avocado, scoop out the flesh
- 1 lime juice
- 2 tbsp green onion
- 1/4 cup cilantro
- 1/4 tsp paprika
- 14.5 oz can chickpeas, drained
- Pepper
- Salt

Directions:

1. Add all ingredients into the blender container. Secure the lid.
2. Start the blending at low speed, then quickly increase to highest speed and blend for 1 minute or until getting a chunky consistency.
3. Serve and enjoy.

Nutritional Value (Amount per Serving):

- Calories 458
- Fat 22 g
- Carbohydrates 57.6 g
- Sugar 1.1 g
- Protein 12.4 g
- Cholesterol 0 mg

Creamy Tomatillo Dressing

Preparation Time: 10 minutes
Cooking Time: 1 minute
Serve: 16

Ingredients:

- 2 tomatillo, husked & chopped
- 1 jalapeno pepper, diced
- 1 lemon juice
- 1 garlic clove
- 1/2 cup cilantro
- 1 cup mayonnaise
- 1 cup buttermilk
- 1 packet ranch seasoning mix

Directions:

1. Add all ingredients into the blender container. Secure the lid.
2. Start the blending at low speed, then quickly increase to highest speed and blend for 1 minute or until smooth.
3. Serve and enjoy.

Nutritional Value (Amount per Serving):

- Calories 66
- Fat 5.1 g
- Carbohydrates 4.7 g
- Sugar 1.8 g
- Protein 0.7 g
- Cholesterol 4 mg

Easy Hollandaise Sauce

Preparation Time: 10 minutes
Cooking Time: 1 minute
Serve: 12

Ingredients:

- 3 egg yolks
- 1/2 cup butter, melted
- 1 tbsp vinegar
- 3/4 tsp dry mustard
- Pepper
- Salt

Directions:

1. Add all ingredients into the blender container. Secure the lid.
2. Start the blending at low speed, then quickly increase to highest speed and blend for 1 minute or until thick & fluffy.
3. Serve and enjoy.

Nutritional Value (Amount per Serving):

- Calories 83
- Fat 8.9 g
- Carbohydrates 0.3 g
- Sugar 0.1 g
- Protein 0.8 g
- Cholesterol 73 mg

Honey Mustard Dressing

Preparation Time: 10 minutes
Cooking Time: 1 minute
Serve: 8

Ingredients:

- 3/4 cup olive oil
- 1/3 cup vinegar
- 2 tbsp lime juice
- 1 garlic clove
- 1/4 cup Dijon mustard
- 1/4 cup honey
- Salt

Directions:

1. Add all ingredients into the blender container. Secure the lid.
2. Start the blending at low speed, then quickly increase to highest speed and blend for 1 minute or until smooth.
3. Serve and enjoy.

Nutritional Value (Amount per Serving):

- Calories 205
- Fat 19.2 g
- Carbohydrates 10.3 g
- Sugar 9 g
- Protein 0.4 g
- Cholesterol 0 mg

Cheese Pepper Spread

Preparation Time: 10 minutes
Cooking Time: 1 minute
Serve: 20

Ingredients:

- 1 cup can roasted red peppers, drained
- 1/4 tsp red chili flakes
- 1 tsp lime juice
- 8 oz cream cheese
- 1 garlic clove
- 1/2 tsp dried basil
- Pepper
- Salt

Directions:

1. Add all ingredients into the blender container. Secure the lid.
2. Start the blending at low speed, then quickly increase to highest speed and blend for 1 minute or until smooth & creamy.
3. Serve and enjoy.

Nutritional Value (Amount per Serving):

- Calories 45
- Fat 4.1 g
- Carbohydrates 1.4 g
- Sugar 0.6 g
- Protein 1 g
- Cholesterol 12 mg

Zesty Chipotle Ranch Dressing

Preparation Time: 10 minutes
Cooking Time: 1 minute
Serve: 6

Ingredients:

- 1 chipotle pepper
- 1/2 tsp dill
- 1/4 tsp onion powder
- 1/2 tsp garlic powder
- 2 tbsp cilantro
- 1 tbsp lime juice
- 1/4 cup buttermilk
- 1/4 cup sour cream
- 1/2 cup mayonnaise
- Pepper
- Salt

Directions:

1. Add all ingredients into the blender container. Secure the lid.
2. Start the blending at low speed, then quickly increase to highest speed and blend for 1 minute or until smooth.
3. Serve and enjoy.

Nutritional Value (Amount per Serving):

- Calories 111
- Fat 8.7 g
- Carbohydrates 8.1 g
- Sugar 2.8 g
- Protein 1.3 g
- Cholesterol 10 mg

Easy Strawberry Dressing

Preparation Time: 10 minutes
Cooking Time: 1 minute
Serve: 4

Ingredients:

- 1 cup fresh strawberries
- 3/4 tbsp honey
- 1 tbsp vinegar
- 3 tbsp olive oil
- Pepper
- Salt

Directions:

1. Add all ingredients into the blender container. Secure the lid.
2. Start the blending at low speed, then quickly increase to highest speed and blend for 1 minute or until smooth.
3. Serve and enjoy.

Nutritional Value (Amount per Serving):

- Calories 114
- Fat 10.6 g
- Carbohydrates 6.1 g
- Sugar 5 g
- Protein 0.3 g
- Cholesterol 0 mg

Chickpea Pepper Spread

Preparation Time: 10 minutes
Cooking Time: 1 minute
Serve: 8

Ingredients:

- 14.5 oz can chickpeas, drained
- 1 tbsp olive oil
- 1/2 tsp paprika
- 1 tbsp vinegar
- 4 oz can roasted red peppers, drained
- Pepper
- Salt

Directions:

1. Add all ingredients into the blender container. Secure the lid.
2. Start the blending at low speed, then quickly increase to highest speed and blend for 1 minute or until smooth & creamy.
3. Serve and enjoy.

Nutritional Value (Amount per Serving):

- Calories 83
- Fat 2.5 g
- Carbohydrates 12.7 g
- Sugar 0.6 g
- Protein 2.7 g
- Cholesterol 0 mg

Chapter 4: Desserts

Easy Lemon Curd

Preparation Time: 5 minutes
Cooking Time: 5 minutes
Serve: 4

Ingredients:

- 5 eggs
- 1/2 cup butter, cut into chunks
- 1 1/2 cups sugar
- 1/2 cup lemon juice
- 1/8 tsp salt

Directions:

1. Add all ingredients into the blender container. Secure the lid.
2. Start the blending at low speed, then slowly increase to the highest speed and blend for 5 minutes.
3. Pour into the container and place in the refrigerator for 2 hours.
4. Serve and enjoy.

Nutritional Value (Amount per Serving):

- Calories 571
- Fat 28.7 g
- Carbohydrates 76.1 g
- Sugar 76.1 g
- Protein 7.4 g
- Cholesterol 266 mg

Raspberry Mousse

Preparation Time: 5 minutes
Cooking Time: 1 minute
Serve: 2

Ingredients:

- 1 cup frozen raspberries
- 1 tbsp almond milk
- 1 frozen banana
- 1 avocado, scoop out the flesh

Directions:

1. Add all ingredients into the blender container. Secure the lid.
2. Start the blending at low speed, then slowly increase to highest speed and blend for 1 minute or until smooth.
3. Pour into the container and place in the refrigerator for 1 hour.
4. Serve and enjoy.

Nutritional Value (Amount per Serving):

- Calories 351
- Fat 21.6 g
- Carbohydrates 41.8 g
- Sugar 28 g
- Protein 3 g
- Cholesterol 0 mg

Peanut Butter Mousse

Preparation Time: 5 minutes
Cooking Time: 5 minutes
Serve: 2

Ingredients:

- 3 tbsp smooth peanut butter
- 1/2 cup chocolate chips
- 1/4 cup sugar
- 14 oz firm tofu, drained & cubed
- 1/2 cup almond milk

Directions:

1. Heat almond milk in a pan until just warm.
2. Add all ingredients into the blender container. Secure the lid.
3. Start the blending at low speed, then slowly increase to highest speed and blend for 1 minute or until smooth.
4. Pour into the container and place in the refrigerator for 4 hours.
5. Serve and enjoy.

Nutritional Value (Amount per Serving):

- Calories 646
- Fat 35.8 g
- Carbohydrates 63 g
- Sugar 54.5 g
- Protein 26.5 g
- Cholesterol 12 mg

Cherry Yogurt

Preparation Time: 5 minutes
Cooking Time: 5 minutes
Serve: 6

Ingredients:

- 16 oz frozen cherries
- 2 tbsp lime juice
- 1 cup plain yogurt
- 1/2 cup maple syrup
- Pinch of salt

Directions:

1. Add all ingredients into the blender container. Secure the lid.
2. Start the blending at low speed, then slowly increase to the highest speed and blend for 5 minutes or until smooth.
3. Pour into the container and place in the refrigerator for 1 hour.
4. Serve and enjoy.

Nutritional Value (Amount per Serving):

- Calories 136
- Fat 0.9 g
- Carbohydrates 30 g
- Sugar 25.6 g
- Protein 3.1 g
- Cholesterol 2 mg

Mango Sorbet

Preparation Time: 5 minutes
Cooking Time: 1 minute
Serve: 5

Ingredients:

- 4 cups mangoes, diced
- 3 cups ice cubes
- 1 cup sugar
- 1 tsp lime juice

Directions:

1. Add all ingredients into the blender container. Secure the lid.
2. Start the blending at low speed, then slowly increase to the highest speed and blend for 5 minutes or until smooth.
3. Serve and enjoy.

Nutritional Value (Amount per Serving):

- Calories 229
- Fat 0.5 g
- Carbohydrates 60.5 g
- Sugar 58.2 g
- Protein 1.1 g
- Cholesterol 0 mg

Strawberry Banana Sorbet

Preparation Time: 5 minutes
Cooking Time: 1 minute
Serve: 6

Ingredients:

- 1/2 lb frozen strawberry
- 1/2 lb frozen banana
- 1/3 cup honey
- 3 tbsp fresh lemon juice

Directions:

1. Add all ingredients into the blender container. Secure the lid.
2. Start the blending at low speed, then slowly increase to highest speed and blend for 1 minute or until smooth.
3. Pour into the container and place in the refrigerator for 3 hours.
4. Serve and enjoy.

Nutritional Value (Amount per Serving):

- Calories 106
- Fat 0.7 g
- Carbohydrates 25.2 g
- Sugar 21.9 g
- Protein 1.2 g
- Cholesterol 3 mg

Chia Chocolate Pudding

Preparation Time: 5 minutes
Cooking Time: 1 minute
Serve: 4

Ingredients:

- 6 tbsp chia seeds
- 1 tsp vanilla
- 2 tbsp cocoa powder
- 1/4 cup honey
- 1 cup almond milk
- Pinch of salt

Directions:

1. Add all ingredients into the blender container. Secure the lid.
2. Start the blending at low speed, then slowly increase to highest speed and blend for 1 minute or until smooth.
3. Pour into the container and place in the refrigerator for 3 hours.
4. Serve and enjoy.

Nutritional Value (Amount per Serving):

- Calories 418
- Fat 27.7 g
- Carbohydrates 40.3 g
- Sugar 19.6 g
- Protein 8.9 g
- Cholesterol 0 mg

Perfect Pineapple Ice Cream

Preparation Time: 5 minutes
Cooking Time: 5 minutes
Serve: 6

Ingredients:

- 20 oz can crushed pineapple
- 1/2 cup heavy cream
- 1 1/2 cups pineapple juice

Directions:

1. Add all ingredients into the blender container. Secure the lid.
2. Start the blending at low speed, then slowly increase to the highest speed and blend for 5 minutes or until smooth.
3. Pour into the container and place in the refrigerator for 4 hours.
4. Serve and enjoy.

Nutritional Value (Amount per Serving):

- Calories 118
- Fat 3.8 g
- Carbohydrates 20.9 g
- Sugar 15.7 g
- Protein 0.8 g
- Cholesterol 14 mg

Easy Pumpkin Mousse

Preparation Time: 5 minutes
Cooking Time: 1 minute
Serve: 4

Ingredients:

- 1/2 cup pumpkin puree
- 1 tsp vanilla
- 1 tbsp pumpkin pie spice
- 1/4 cup maple syrup
- 1 cup coconut cream
- Pinch of salt

Directions:

1. Add all ingredients into the blender container. Secure the lid.
2. Start the blending at low speed, then slowly increase to highest speed and blend for 1 minute or until smooth.
3. Pour into the container and place in the refrigerator for 2 hours.
4. Serve and enjoy.

Nutritional Value (Amount per Serving):

- Calories 208
- Fat 14.6 g
- Carbohydrates 20.1 g
- Sugar 15 g
- Protein 1.8 g
- Cholesterol 0 mg

Pumpkin Mousse

Preparation Time: 5 minutes
Cooking Time: 1 minute
Serve: 10

Ingredients:

- 15 oz can pumpkin puree
- 3/4 cup heavy cream
- 2 tbsp pumpkin spice
- 2 tsp vanilla
- 1/2 cup Swerve
- 12 oz cream cheese, softened

Directions:

1. Add all ingredients into the blender container. Secure the lid.
2. Start the blending at low speed, then slowly increase to highest speed and blend for 1 minute or until smooth.
3. Pour into the container and place in the refrigerator for 2 hours.
4. Serve and enjoy.

Nutritional Value (Amount per Serving):

- Calories 219
- Fat 15.3 g
- Carbohydrates 17.1 g
- Sugar 6.3 g
- Protein 4.3 g
- Cholesterol 50 mg

Blueberry Sorbet

Preparation Time: 5 minutes
Cooking Time: 1 minute
Serve: 4

Ingredients:

- 4 cups frozen blueberries
- 1/2 cup water
- 2 tbsp honey

Directions:

1. Add all ingredients into the blender container. Secure the lid.
2. Start the blending at low speed, then slowly increase to highest speed and blend for 1 minute or until smooth.
3. Pour into the container and place in the refrigerator for 4 hours.
4. Serve and enjoy.

Nutritional Value (Amount per Serving):

- Calories 115
- Fat 0.5 g
- Carbohydrates 29.7 g
- Sugar 23 g
- Protein 1.1 g
- Cholesterol 0 mg

Easy Cherry Sorbet

Preparation Time: 5 minutes
Cooking Time: 1 minute
Serve: 6

Ingredients:

- 1 lb frozen cherries, pitted
- 1 tsp fresh lemon juice
- 1 cup sugar

Directions:

1. Add all ingredients into the blender container. Secure the lid.
2. Start the blending at low speed, then slowly increase to highest speed and blend for 1 minute or until smooth.
3. Pour into the container and place in the refrigerator for 5 hours.
4. Serve and enjoy.

Nutritional Value (Amount per Serving):

- Calories 160
- Fat 0.3 g
- Carbohydrates 41.7 g
- Sugar 40.2 g
- Protein 0.7 g
- Cholesterol 0 mg

Nutella Banana Ice Cream

Preparation Time: 5 minutes
Cooking Time: 1 minute
Serve: 4

Ingredients:

- 4 frozen banana
- 1/2 cup Nutella

Directions:

1. Add all ingredients into the blender container. Secure the lid.
2. Start the blending at low speed, then slowly increase to highest speed and blend for 1 minute or until smooth.
3. Pour into the container and place in the refrigerator for 2 hours.
4. Serve and enjoy.

Nutritional Value (Amount per Serving):

- Calories 135
- Fat 3.4 g
- Carbohydrates 22.9 g
- Sugar 17.5 g
- Protein 3.3 g
- Cholesterol 10 mg

Peach Ice Cream

Preparation Time: 5 minutes
Cooking Time: 1 minute
Serve: 4

Ingredients:

- 3 cups frozen peach slices
- 2 tbsp honey
- 1 1/2 cups almond milk

Directions:

1. Add all ingredients into the blender container. Secure the lid.
2. Start the blending at low speed, then slowly increase to highest speed and blend for 1 minute or until smooth.
3. Pour into the container and place in the refrigerator for 4 hours.
4. Serve and enjoy.

Nutritional Value (Amount per Serving):

- Calories 415
- Fat 21.7 g
- Carbohydrates 58.6 g
- Sugar 53.2 g
- Protein 3.3 g
- Cholesterol 0 mg

Raspberry Sorbet

Preparation Time: 5 minutes
Cooking Time: 1 minute
Serve: 2

Ingredients:

- 1/2 cup frozen cherries, pitted
- 1 1/3 cups frozen raspberries
- 1 frozen banana
- 2/3 cup almond milk

Directions:

1. Add all ingredients into the blender container. Secure the lid.
2. Start the blending at low speed, then slowly increase to highest speed and blend for 1 minute or until smooth.
3. Serve and enjoy.

Nutritional Value (Amount per Serving):

- Calories 429
- Fat 20.5 g
- Carbohydrates 62.3 g
- Sugar 49.9 g
- Protein 4.9 g
- Cholesterol 5 mg

Pineapple Mango Sorbet

Preparation Time: 5 minutes
Cooking Time: 1 minute
Serve: 4

Ingredients:

- 2 cups frozen pineapple
- 2 cups frozen mango
- 1 tbsp maple syrup

Directions:

1. Add all ingredients into the blender container. Secure the lid.
2. Start the blending at low speed, then slowly increase to highest speed and blend for 1 minute or until smooth.
3. Serve and enjoy.

Nutritional Value (Amount per Serving):

- Calories 178
- Fat 2.6 g
- Carbohydrates 37.3 g
- Sugar 32.7 g
- Protein 2.5 g
- Cholesterol 10 mg

Strawberry Cheesecake Ice Cream

Preparation Time: 5 minutes
Cooking Time: 1 minute
Serve: 2

Ingredients:

- 1 cup frozen strawberries
- 6 drops liquid stevia
- 1 tbsp cream cheese
- 1/4 cup greek yogurt
- 3/4 cup almond milk

Directions:

1. Add all ingredients into the blender container. Secure the lid.
2. Start the blending at low speed, then slowly increase to highest speed and blend for 1 minute or until smooth.
3. Serve and enjoy.

Nutritional Value (Amount per Serving):

- Calories 268
- Fat 23.7 g
- Carbohydrates 12.6 g
- Sugar 8.5 g
- Protein 5 g
- Cholesterol 7 mg

Orange Pineapple Sorbet

Preparation Time: 5 minutes
Cooking Time: 1 minute
Serve: 4

Ingredients:

- 1/2 orange zest
- 3 cups frozen pineapple chunks

Directions:

1. Add all ingredients into the blender container. Secure the lid.
2. Start the blending at low speed, then slowly increase to highest speed and blend for 1 minute or until smooth.
3. Pour into the container and place in the refrigerator for 4 hours.
4. Serve and enjoy.

Nutritional Value (Amount per Serving):

- Calories 159
- Fat 0.2 g
- Carbohydrates 41 g
- Sugar 38.8 g
- Protein 0.8 g
- Cholesterol 0 mg

Yummy Blueberry Yogurt

Preparation Time: 5 minutes
Cooking Time: 1 minute
Serve: 2

Ingredients:

- 1 cup frozen blueberries
- 1 tsp vanilla
- 2 tbsp maple syrup
- 1 1/2 cups almond milk yogurt
- Pinch of salt

Directions:

1. Add all ingredients into the blender container. Secure the lid.
2. Start the blending at low speed, then slowly increase to highest speed and blend for 1 minute or until smooth.
3. Serve and enjoy.

Nutritional Value (Amount per Serving):

- Calories 212
- Fat 4.8 g
- Carbohydrates 42.2 g
- Sugar 32.9 g
- Protein 2.8 g
- Cholesterol 0 mg

Coconut Cherry Popsicles

Preparation Time: 5 minutes
Cooking Time: 1 minute
Serve: 10

Ingredients:

- 14 oz can full-fat coconut milk
- 1 tsp maple syrup
- 2 cups fresh cherries, pitted

Directions:

1. Add all ingredients into the blender container. Secure the lid.
2. Start the blending at low speed, then slowly increase to highest speed and blend for 1 minute or until smooth.
3. Pour into the popsicle molds and place in refrigerator until set.
4. Serve and enjoy.

Nutritional Value (Amount per Serving):

- Calories 92
- Fat 7.3 g
- Carbohydrates 5.8 g
- Sugar 1 g
- Protein 0.7 g
- Cholesterol 0 mg

Chapter 5: Drinks

Thick & Creamy Banana Smoothie

Preparation Time: 5 minutes
Cooking Time: 1 minute
Serve: 2

Ingredients:

- 2 bananas
- 2 tbsp maple syrup
- 1/2 cup almond milk
- 1 cup Greek yogurt

Directions:

1. Add all ingredients into the blender container. Secure the lid.
2. Start the blending on low speed, then quickly increase to highest speed and blend for 1 minute or until smooth.
3. Serve and enjoy.

Nutritional Value (Amount per Serving):

- Calories 295
- Fat 14.7 g
- Carbohydrates 43.7 g
- Sugar 28.3 g
- Protein 2.7 g
- Cholesterol 0 mg

Banana Coffee Smoothie

Preparation Time: 5 minutes
Cooking Time: 1 minute
Serve: 2

Ingredients:

- 1 cup brewed coffee
- 1 tbsp cocoa powder
- 1 cup milk
- 1 tbsp almond butter
- 1 banana

Directions:

1. Add all ingredients into the blender container. Secure the lid.
2. Start the blending on low speed, then quickly increase to highest speed and blend for 1 minute or until smooth.
3. Serve and enjoy.

Nutritional Value (Amount per Serving):

- Calories 170
- Fat 7.6 g
- Carbohydrates 22.5 g
- Sugar 13.1 g
- Protein 7 g
- Cholesterol 10 mg

Cinnamon Banana Smoothie

Preparation Time: 5 minutes
Cooking Time: 1 minute
Serve: 2

Ingredients:

- 1 banana
- 1/2 cup ice
- 1/8 tsp cinnamon
- 1/3 tsp vanilla
- 1/4 cup walnuts
- 1/3 cup rolled oats
- 1 cup almond milk
- 1 apple, peel & dice
- Pinch of salt

Directions:

1. Add all ingredients into the blender container. Secure the lid.
2. Start the blending on low speed, then quickly increase to highest speed and blend for 1 minute or until smooth.
3. Serve and enjoy.

Nutritional Value (Amount per Serving):

- Calories 537
- Fat 39.1 g
- Carbohydrates 46 g
- Sugar 23 g
- Protein 9.3 g
- Cholesterol 0 mg

Healthy Berry Smoothie

Preparation Time: 5 minutes
Cooking Time: 1 minute
Serve: 2

Ingredients:

- 1/2 cup blueberries
- 1 cup strawberries
- 1 tbsp honey
- 1 cup almond milk
- 1 tbsp chia seeds
- 1/3 cup oats

Directions:

1. Add all ingredients into the blender container. Secure the lid.
2. Start the blending on low speed, then quickly increase to highest speed and blend for 1 minute or until smooth.
3. Serve and enjoy.

Nutritional Value (Amount per Serving):

- Calories 403
- Fat 29.9 g
- Carbohydrates 35.3 g
- Sugar 19.9 g
- Protein 5.3 g
- Cholesterol 0 mg

Healthy Avocado Spinach Smoothie

Preparation Time: 5 minutes
Cooking Time: 1 minute
Serve: 2

Ingredients:

- 2 cups spinach
- 3/4 cup almond milk
- 1 tbsp almond butter
- 1/2 avocado, scoop out the flesh
- 1 banana

Directions:

1. Add all ingredients into the blender container. Secure the lid.
2. Start the blending on low speed, then quickly increase to highest speed and blend for 1 minute or until smooth.
3. Serve and enjoy.

Nutritional Value (Amount per Serving):

- Calories 418
- Fat 36.1 g
- Carbohydrates 25.4 g
- Sugar 11 g
- Protein 6.2 g
- Cholesterol 0 mg

Easy Strawberry Protein Shake

Preparation Time: 5 minutes
Cooking Time: 1 minute
Serve: 2

Ingredients:

- 8 strawberries
- 5 drops liquid stevia
- 1 tsp vanilla
- 2 1/2 cups almond milk
- 2 scoops whey protein powder

Directions:

1. Add all ingredients into the blender container. Secure the lid.
2. Start the blending on low speed, then quickly increase to highest speed and blend for 1 minute or until smooth.
3. Serve and enjoy.

Nutritional Value (Amount per Serving):

- Calories 216
- Fat 5 g
- Carbohydrates 17 g
- Sugar 11 g
- Protein 23 g
- Cholesterol 65 mg

Green Pineapple Smoothie

Preparation Time: 5 minutes
Cooking Time: 1 minute
Serve: 2

Ingredients:

- 1/2 cup pineapple
- 1 banana
- 1/2 cup mango
- 2 cups spinach
- 1 cup almond milk
- 1 cup Greek yogurt

Directions:

1. Add all ingredients into the blender container. Secure the lid.
2. Start the blending on low speed, then quickly increase to highest speed and blend for 1 minute or until smooth.
3. Serve and enjoy.

Nutritional Value (Amount per Serving):

- Calories 381
- Fat 29.1 g
- Carbohydrates 32.8 g
- Sugar 21.1 g
- Protein 4.8 g
- Cholesterol 0 mg

Watermelon Strawberry Smoothie

Preparation Time: 5 minutes
Cooking Time: 1 minute
Serve: 2

Ingredients:

- 3 1/2 cups watermelon
- 8 oz strawberries

Directions:

1. Add all ingredients into the blender container. Secure the lid.
2. Start the blending on low speed, then quickly increase to highest speed and blend for 1 minute or until smooth.
3. Serve and enjoy.

Nutritional Value (Amount per Serving):

- Calories 116
- Fat 0.7 g
- Carbohydrates 28.7 g
- Sugar 21 g
- Protein 2.3 g
- Cholesterol 0 mg

Mango Strawberry Smoothie

Preparation Time: 5 minutes
Cooking Time: 1 minute
Serve: 2

Ingredients:

- 1/2 cup strawberry
- 1/2 cup mango
- 1 tbsp honey
- 1 cup orange juice
- 3 tbsp water
- 3/4 cup orange juice

Directions:

1. Add all ingredients into the blender container. Secure the lid.
2. Start the blending on low speed, then quickly increase to highest speed and blend for 1 minute or until smooth.
3. Serve and enjoy.

Nutritional Value (Amount per Serving):

- Calories 166
- Fat 0.7 g
- Carbohydrates 40.2 g
- Sugar 34.2 g
- Protein 2.1 g
- Cholesterol 0 mg

Easy Pineapple Lemonade

Preparation Time: 5 minutes
Cooking Time: 1 minute
Serve: 2

Ingredients:

- 2 cups pineapple chunks
- 1 cup ice cubes
- 1 lemon juice

Directions:

1. Add all ingredients into the blender container. Secure the lid.
2. Start the blending on low speed, then quickly increase to highest speed and blend for 1 minute or until smooth.
3. Serve and enjoy.

Nutritional Value (Amount per Serving):

- Calories 82
- Fat 0.2 g
- Carbohydrates 21.7 g
- Sugar 16.3 g
- Protein 0.9 g
- Cholesterol 0 mg

Kiwi Strawberry Smoothie

Preparation Time: 5 minutes
Cooking Time: 1 minute
Serve: 2

Ingredients:

- 2 cups strawberries
- 1/2 tsp vanilla
- 1 cup almond milk
- 1 banana
- 2 kiwi, peeled & diced

Directions:

1. Add all ingredients into the blender container. Secure the lid.
2. Start the blending on low speed, then quickly increase to highest speed and blend for 1 minute or until smooth.
3. Serve and enjoy.

Nutritional Value (Amount per Serving):

- Calories 424
- Fat 29 g
- Carbohydrates 42 g
- Sugar 25 g
- Protein 5 g
- Cholesterol 0 mg

Spinach Cucumber Smoothie

Preparation Time: 5 minutes
Cooking Time: 1 minute
Serve: 4

Ingredients:

- 1 avocado, scoop out the flesh
- 1 cucumber
- 1 1/2 cups spinach
- 1 apple, diced
- 4 dates, pitted
- 2 cups almond milk

Directions:

1. Add all ingredients into the blender container. Secure the lid.
2. Start the blending on low speed, then quickly increase to highest speed and blend for 1 minute or until smooth.
3. Serve and enjoy.

Nutritional Value (Amount per Serving):

- Calories 445
- Fat 38 g
- Carbohydrates 28 g
- Sugar 16 g
- Protein 4.9 g
- Cholesterol 0 mg

Healthy Tropical Smoothie

Preparation Time: 5 minutes
Cooking Time: 1 minute
Serve: 2

Ingredients:

- 1/2 cup pineapple
- 1/2 cup mango
- 1/2 banana
- 1 tbsp orange juice
- 1/2 cup coconut milk

Directions:

1. Add all ingredients into the blender container. Secure the lid.
2. Start the blending on low speed, then quickly increase to highest speed and blend for 1 minute or until smooth.
3. Serve and enjoy.

Nutritional Value (Amount per Serving):

- Calories 213
- Fat 14.6 g
- Carbohydrates 22.5 g
- Sugar 16 g
- Protein 2.3 g
- Cholesterol 0 mg

Banana Peanut Butter Smoothie

Preparation Time: 5 minutes
Cooking Time: 1 minute
Serve: 2

Ingredients:

- 1 1/2 cups almond milk
- 1 cup ice
- 1 tbsp cocoa powder
- 1/2 tsp vanilla
- 2 tbsp Greek yogurt
- 2 tbsp peanut butter
- 2 bananas

Directions:

1. Add all ingredients into the blender container. Secure the lid.
2. Start the blending on low speed, then quickly increase to highest speed and blend for 1 minute or until smooth.
3. Serve and enjoy.

Nutritional Value (Amount per Serving):

- Calories 622
- Fat 51 g
- Carbohydrates 41 g
- Sugar 22 g
- Protein 9 g
- Cholesterol 0 mg

Creamy Strawberry Milkshake

Preparation Time: 5 minutes
Cooking Time: 1 minute
Serve: 2

Ingredients:

- 1/2 lb strawberries
- 1/2 cup milk
- 1 tsp vanilla
- 2 cups vanilla ice cream
- 1 1/2 tbsp sugar

Directions:

1. Add all ingredients into the blender container. Secure the lid.
2. Start the blending on low speed, then quickly increase to highest speed and blend for 1 minute or until smooth.
3. Serve and enjoy.

Nutritional Value (Amount per Serving):

- Calories 244
- Fat 8.6 g
- Carbohydrates 37 g
- Sugar 31 g
- Protein 5 g
- Cholesterol 34 mg

Banana Kiwi Smoothie

Preparation Time: 5 minutes
Cooking Time: 1 minute
Serve: 2

Ingredients:

- 1 banana
- 1 cup ice cubes
- 1 cup Greek yogurt
- 1 lime juice
- 1/2 cup almond milk
- 2 kiwi, peel & chopped

Directions:

1. Add all ingredients into the blender container. Secure the lid.
2. Start the blending on low speed, then quickly increase to highest speed and blend for 1 minute or until smooth.
3. Serve and enjoy.

Nutritional Value (Amount per Serving):

- Calories 237
- Fat 14.9 g
- Carbohydrates 27 g
- Sugar 16 g
- Protein 2.9 g
- Cholesterol 0 mg

Peach Lemonade

Preparation Time: 5 minutes
Cooking Time: 1 minute
Serve: 2

Ingredients:

- 2 cups peach slices
- 1 cup ice cubes
- 2 lemon juice
- 1/4 cup sugar

Directions:

1. Add all ingredients into the blender container. Secure the lid.
2. Start the blending on low speed, then quickly increase to highest speed and blend for 1 minute or until desired consistency.
3. Serve and enjoy.

Nutritional Value (Amount per Serving):

- Calories 153
- Fat 0.4 g
- Carbohydrates 39 g
- Sugar 39 g
- Protein 1.4 g
- Cholesterol 0 mg

Mango Pineapple Peach Smoothie

Preparation Time: 5 minutes
Cooking Time: 1 minute
Serve: 2

Ingredients:

- 1/2 cup mango
- 1/2 cup pineapple
- 1/2 cup peaches
- 2 tbsp protein powder
- 1/2 tbsp honey
- 1 tbsp ginger, grated
- 3/4 cup coconut milk
- 1/2 tbsp lemon zest
- 1 lemon juice

Directions:

1. Add all ingredients into the blender container. Secure the lid.
2. Start the blending on low speed, then quickly increase to highest speed and blend for 1 minute or until smooth.
3. Serve and enjoy.

Nutritional Value (Amount per Serving):

- Calories 293
- Fat 21 g
- Carbohydrates 26 g
- Sugar 20 g
- Protein 3 g
- Cholesterol 0 mg

Cookie Shake

Preparation Time: 5 minutes
Cooking Time: 1 minute
Serve: 1

Ingredients:

- 1 chocolate graham cracker, crushed
- 1/2 cup almond milk
- 1 1/2 cups ice cubes
- 1 scoop chocolate protein powder
- Pinch of salt

Directions:

1. Add all ingredients into the blender container. Secure the lid.
2. Start the blending on low speed, then quickly increase to highest speed and blend for 1 minute or until smooth.
3. Serve and enjoy.

Nutritional Value (Amount per Serving):

- Calories 399
- Fat 32 g
- Carbohydrates 18 g
- Sugar 10 g
- Protein 13 g
- Cholesterol 20 mg

Healthy Raspberry Smoothie

Preparation Time: 5 minutes
Cooking Time: 1 minute
Serve: 2

Ingredients:

- 2 cups raspberries
- 1 cup yogurt
- 1 cup almond milk
- 1 lime juice
- 1 lime zest
- 1 tbsp honey

Directions:

1. Add all ingredients into the blender container. Secure the lid.
2. Start the blending on low speed, then quickly increase to highest speed and blend for 1 minute or until smooth.
3. Serve and enjoy.

Nutritional Value (Amount per Serving):

- Calories 459
- Fat 30.9 g
- Carbohydrates 38.6 g
- Sugar 26.7 g
- Protein 11.2 g
- Cholesterol 7 mg

Watermelon Strawberry Smoothie

Preparation Time: 5 minutes
Cooking Time: 1 minute
Serve: 2

Ingredients:

- 1 tbsp hemp seeds
- 3/4 cup yogurt
- 1 cup strawberries
- 4 cups watermelon

Directions:

1. Add all ingredients into the blender container. Secure the lid.
2. Start the blending on low speed, then quickly increase to highest speed and blend for 1 minute or until smooth.
3. Serve and enjoy.

Nutritional Value (Amount per Serving):

- Calories 180
- Fat 1.7 g
- Carbohydrates 34.8 g
- Sugar 28.7 g
- Protein 7.5 g
- Cholesterol 6 mg

Healthy Orange Smoothie

Preparation Time: 5 minutes
Cooking Time: 1 minute
Serve: 1

Ingredients:

- 1 cup orange juice
- 1/2 cup carrots, chopped
- 1/2 tsp turmeric
- 1 tsp ginger, minced
- 1 banana

Directions:

1. Add all ingredients into the blender container. Secure the lid.
2. Start the blending on low speed, then quickly increase to highest speed and blend for 1 minute or until smooth.
3. Serve and enjoy.

Nutritional Value (Amount per Serving):

- Calories 250
- Fat 1.1 g
- Carbohydrates 60.1 g
- Sugar 38 g
- Protein 3.7 g
- Cholesterol 0 mg

Creamy Cherry Smoothie

Preparation Time: 5 minutes
Cooking Time: 1 minute
Serve: 2

Ingredients:

- 1 1/2 cups cherries
- 1 cup Greek yogurt
- 1 banana
- 1 1/2 cups apple juice

Directions:

1. Add all ingredients into the blender container. Secure the lid.
2. Start the blending on low speed, then quickly increase to highest speed and blend for 1 minute or until smooth.
3. Serve and enjoy.

Nutritional Value (Amount per Serving):

- Calories 163
- Fat 0.6 g
- Carbohydrates 40 g
- Sugar 29 g
- Protein 1.3 g
- Cholesterol 0 mg

Spinach Cherry Banana Smoothie

Preparation Time: 5 minutes
Cooking Time: 1 minute
Serve: 2

Ingredients:

- 1 cup spinach
- 1 cup frozen cherries
- 1 banana
- 1/2 cup ice
- 1 cup almond milk

Directions:

1. Add all ingredients into the blender container. Secure the lid.
2. Start the blending on low speed, then quickly increase to highest speed and blend for 1 minute or until smooth.
3. Serve and enjoy.

Nutritional Value (Amount per Serving):

- Calories 368
- Fat 29 g
- Carbohydrates 29 g
- Sugar 18 g
- Protein 4 g
- Cholesterol 0 mg

Cinnamon Apple Smoothie

Preparation Time: 5 minutes
Cooking Time: 1 minute
Serve: 2

Ingredients:

- 2 apples, sliced
- 1 cup ice cubes
- 3/4 tsp ground cinnamon
- 1/2 tsp vanilla
- 1 1/2 tbsp chia seeds
- 2 tbsp almond butter
- 1/3 cup rolled oats
- 1 1/2 cups almond milk

Directions:

1. Add all ingredients into the blender container. Secure the lid.
2. Start the blending on low speed, then quickly increase to highest speed and blend for 1 minute or until smooth.
3. Serve and enjoy.

Nutritional Value (Amount per Serving):

- Calories 685
- Fat 53 g
- Carbohydrates 53 g
- Sugar 30 g
- Protein 9 g
- Cholesterol 0 mg